Transforming the Remote Work Experience

Bring the in-office experiences to remote work using Microsoft Teams

Melanie Gass

Copyright © 2020 by Melanie Gass

All rights reserved. This book or any portion thereof may not be reproduced or used in any manner whatsoever without the express written permission of the publisher except for the use of brief quotations in a book review or scholarly journal.

First Printing: 2020

ISBN 978-1-7350535-0-9

www.transformremotework.com

NOTICES
While the author takes care to ensure the accuracy and quality of these materials, we cannot guarantee their accuracy, and all materials are provided without any warranty whatsoever; including, but not limited to, the implied warranties of merchantability or fitness for a particular purpose. Use of screenshots, photographs of another entity's products, or another entity's product name or service is for illustrative purposes only and are the property of the software proprietor.

Microsoft is a either a registered trademark or trademark of Microsoft Corporation in the United States and/or other countries.

Microsoft Teams is a registered trademark of Microsoft Corporation in the United States and other countries; the Microsoft Corporation products and services discussed or described may be trademarks of Microsoft Corporation. All other product names and services used throughout the book may be common law or registered trademarks of their respective proprietors.

Microsoft screenshots and icons used with permission from Microsoft Corporation as described for training manual, documentation and tutorial use.

Ios is a registered trademark of Cisco Corporation in the United States and/or other counties.

Ipad is a registered trademark of Apple Corporation in the United States and/or other counties.

Android is a registered trademark of Google LLC in the United States and/or other counties.

This book conveys no rights in the software or other products about which it was written; all use or licensing of such software or other products is the responsibility of the user according to terms and conditions of the owner. Do not make illegal copies of books. If you believe this book, related or other Melanie Gass materials are being transmitted without permission, please email info@melaniegass.com.

Dedication

This is for everyone who has realized it's time embrace change. Thank you for your courage to try it.

Table of Contents

Introduction	11
Chapter 1: The Remote Box	13
Chapter 2: Knock on the Door	19
Chapter 3: Attend an In-Person Meeting	21
Chapter 4: Host an In-Person Meeting	25
Chapter 5: One to One Meetings	29
Chapter 6: Hallway conversation	35
Chapter 7: Open office space	39
Chapter 8: Coffee or Lunch breaks	43
Chapter 9: Morale Event	47
Chapter 10: Best Practice Tips	51
Notes	55

Introduction

Years ago, mobile telephones were the size of a brick and only made phone calls. Today, the mobile phone fits in the palm of your hand can replace your laptop. These advanced capabilities show us that technology changes rapidly, but it's our shift as a culture to meet it that means the most.

At one time, we commuted to an office. We worked side by side, saw one another every day and discussed television episodes around the proverbial water cooler. Over time, our culture shifted with technology adoption and today it's evolved to a new normal of blended work and friendship lines with co-workers from around the world staying connected through video and social media.

This guide is designed for those who are looking to mirror the comforts of the connected life you are used to in person through a remote working environment. I wrote this book based on my own experiences as an employee and business owner throughout my career to create a relatable experience you may be familiar with. This book translates the in-person experience to a guided approach leveraging Microsoft Teams for the remote working platform. While I've used many remote technologies and trained others on them over the years, I chose Microsoft Teams due to the robust platform of options to make your day more productive in addition to feeling connected to others. For the intentions of this guide though, we'll focus on creating a new comfort using this digital space.

As you venture into this uncharted territory, my hope is that you find comfort working in a remote environment to stay connected and shift your life in a positive way.

Chapter 1: The Remote Box

I first launched Microsoft Teams while sitting in an open working space at a desk. As Microsoft Teams opened, I watched a large purple box fill the screen with my typical wide-eyed curious stare. "This looks like a box" I said to myself.

As a examined the box, I noticed a simple purple square outline with white icons vertically on the left. There are icon names for activity, chat, teams, calendar, calls and files. Across the top there's a search bar, a circle with my initials and a smaller green dot and checkmark. The usual screen minimize, maximize and close options I'm used to from other programs appear in their usual place on the top right of the screen. Below the top line along the left, there's a square with my initials and a bold name titled general with additional names of posts, files and wiki.

The center looks blank. There are options to add people, create more channels and open FAQ. Below that, there's an option to type as you would find in a chat window, but it looks like I'm not in a chat because on the left side the icon teams is highlighted and chat is not.

I continue to stare and absorb this box for another moment, and it clicks that this box is meant to collaborate with others you work with without having to leave the box. My thoughts of excitement grow as I consider all the ways that we interact with co-workers. We instant message, we share files, we meet on items in a conference room, and for large projects we send mail with notifications of updates and statuses.

I realized the power this app provides. We can replace the email trails that may forget someone with document attachments that require scouring to find while trying to remember who it was that sent it. I remembered the countless times that I've sat in a conference room with someone who sends a file to me so I can edit and return it. That could be replaced using Teams. The number of reply all add-ons to a thread that fill my mailbox could be replaced with this. My instant message and phone apps could be replaced by this. In examining further, it looks like I can find something quickly with search, and that may be faster than looking within mail for a file or info sent a couple of weeks ago in instant message. I concluded that this is a promising option for the future.

Icon Features Overview:

|  | Notifications of someone liking a post, tagging you in a post or chat, adding you to a Team. A number in a red circle will appear when you have a notification. |

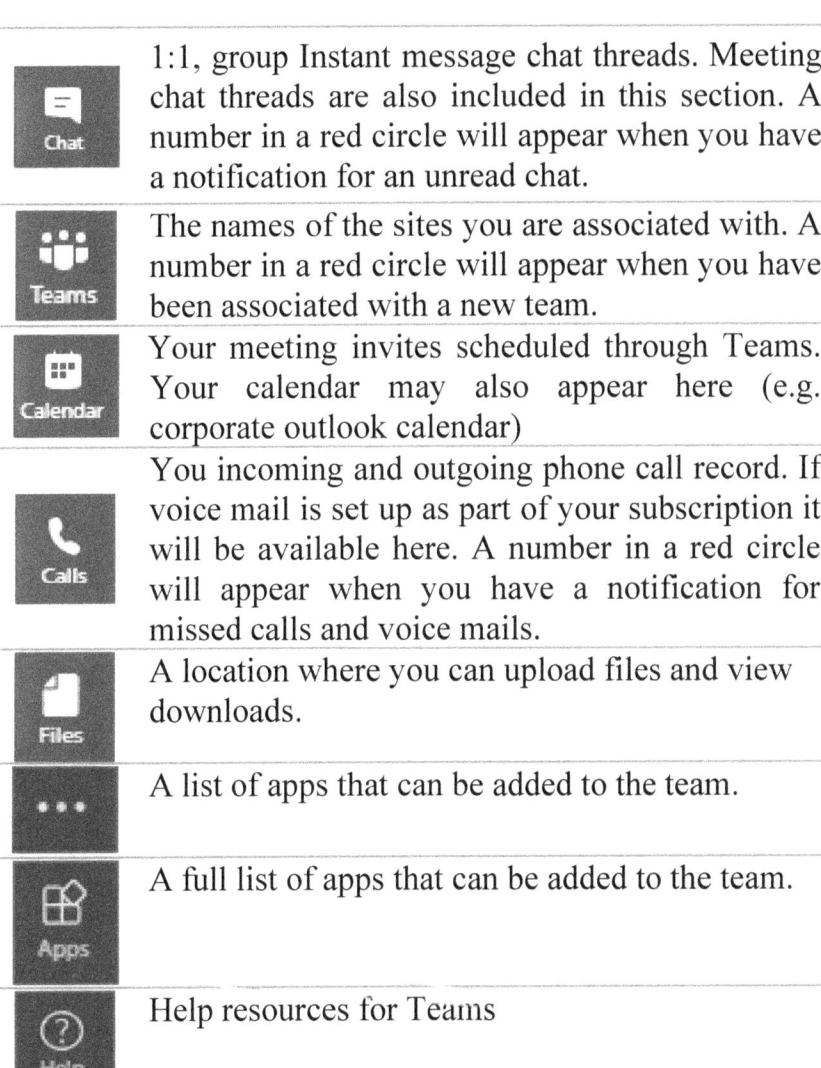

Chat	1:1, group Instant message chat threads. Meeting chat threads are also included in this section. A number in a red circle will appear when you have a notification for an unread chat.
Teams	The names of the sites you are associated with. A number in a red circle will appear when you have been associated with a new team.
Calendar	Your meeting invites scheduled through Teams. Your calendar may also appear here (e.g. corporate outlook calendar)
Calls	You incoming and outgoing phone call record. If voice mail is set up as part of your subscription it will be available here. A number in a red circle will appear when you have a notification for missed calls and voice mails.
Files	A location where you can upload files and view downloads.
...	A list of apps that can be added to the team.
Apps	A full list of apps that can be added to the team.
Help	Help resources for Teams
	Download the mobile app. Available for iOS and Android operating systems.

Default Tab Names:

General	The name in bold will show the name of the channel you are on.

Posts	This is a thread that for posts to alert others. It could be a project status or announcement. Think of it as something you would normally send within an email.
Files	Shared files for others associated with the team to view and edit.
Wiki	A blank page with a subject line and text. You can have multiple sections and pages.

Teams and Channels:

Team Name	A list of your Teams will appear.
General	Channels are listed beneath each team named you are associated with. Think of a channel as a folder where dedicated posts and files related to that channel are available. General is listed as the first channel for each team.

Be Fearless Test:
1. Launch Microsoft Teams to view your remote box.
2. Select each feature along the left side of the screen to become familiar with the view and options.
3. Select each tab to become familiar with the view and options.
4. Select a Team and channel to become familiar with the view and options.

It's possible that your remote box was set up by someone in your IT department ahead of time. Pre-populated information including posts, files and multiple teams may appear.

Chapter 2: Knock on the Door

I typically work within four walls, and there's a door separating my space from the hall. Next to the door is a small vertical pane of glass, and I often think it resembles a fishbowl for those who walk by. As I watch onlookers that walk by through my peripheral vision, some stop and make the phone sign next to their face to ask nonverbally if I'm on a call or knock throughout the day. I wave them in.

"Are you on a call?" they ask. I say no. They proceed to ask their question, say hello and inquire on the weekend, or inform of a business update. The length of time is typically short, averaging between 2-15 minutes.

In remote work, I find a close replacement to the knock in Microsoft Teams by sending an instant message. The glass pane is replaced by an availability status to know if someone is available, busy or away. The knock on the door is replaced by the initial message with the words "are you free?" or "have a minute?" The discussion in person is replaced by an audio or video call depending on time of day and how well we know one another.

Status options:

⊘ Available ● Busy ⊘ Do not disturb ◐ Be right back ⊘ Appear away	Status options will appear next to someone's name using the same colors and symbols shown in the left. As you move over the photo or name of the person, additional details such a "In a call" or "In a meeting" may appear.

19

Icon Features Overview:

 1:1, group Instant message chat threads. Meeting chat threads are also included in this section. A number in a red circle will appear when you have a notification for an unread chat.

Call options:

 Video call. Requires a laptop camera or external camera (or phone camera if you are on a mobile device)

 Phone call. A Teams call is an internet call (think Skype). If a phone number is listed, a phone bridge is connected by your company and available to use.

Be Fearless Test:
1. Select **Chat** from the left side of the screen.
2. At the top of the screen, select the ▧ for a new chat.
3. Begin to type the name of the person. You may see their name populate automatically. Select the name to confirm.
4. At the bottom of the screen, type your message. When complete, select the ▷ .
5. Once you receive a reply, use the video or phone options at the top right of the chat screen to contact based on preference.

 Have a favorite colleague? Once a chat is sent, you can select the ... next to their name and select "Add to favorite contacts." Their name will appear within the "Contacts" section at the top of the chat screen for future convenience.

Chapter 3: Attend an In-Person Meeting

I attend multiple meetings in person throughout the day. When I walk into a room for the meeting, it seems like it's always a different size room. Some are small and hold a few people, others hold fifteen people, and then there are larger room or auditoriums to hold hundreds of people. No matter the room size, I find myself frequently walking the into meeting room to others engaged in small talk while waiting for the meeting host or presenter. I join the conversations related to weekend plans, sports scores and player trades, workstream updates on an initiative, and last night's antics from children.

I feel like my name should be "Sorry I'm late" because I think I must say it as many times as my name every day. I run late for pretty much every meeting because the last meeting never ends early, and the next one I'm late for is in a different room, floor or building.

As a company culture, over the years I've noticed companies have a variety of built-in grace periods. Some companies around the globe I've worked with are laser-focused on time management and it's frowned upon to arrive late. Others extend to five minutes. There was company I remember in the past owned by a household name who was publicly known for being strict, and it was a standard assumption that everyone was ten minutes late to meetings. I found it surprising!

In thinking about how this experience can translate to remote working, there is an opportunity through video calls using Microsoft Teams. It may save the walk between rooms, floors and buildings but meetings still tend run a few minutes late and the small talk remains.

Icons features overview:

 Your meeting invites scheduled through Teams. Your calendar may also appear here (e.g. corporate outlook calendar)

Join the meeting options:

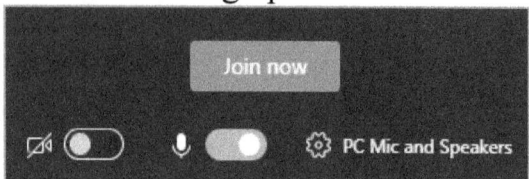

Call options during the meeting:

 Video call show and hide. When a line is through this icon you are not showing video. You can show and hide video at any time during the meeting.

 Phone call audio speak and mute. When a line is through this icon you are muted. You'll often find words above this icon stating "your microphone is muted" when speaking while muted as a reminder. You can speak and mute at any time during the meeting.

 Chat. You can enter text or paste a link during the meeting to keep it related to the meeting and avoid sending as a follow up email.

 Hang up.

 More options. Meeting notes taken during the meeting will appear here.

Whiteboard Function:

Whiteboard	The Whiteboard appears at the top of the screen in the chat section for the meeting within 1 more. You can always refer to these after the meeting by selecting the name of meeting in the chat section.

Meeting Notes Function:

Notes Capture meeting objectives, important notes or action items	Meeting notes can be individual or grouped together.
Meeting Notes	Meeting notes appear at the top of the screen in the chat section for the meeting. You can always refer to these after the meeting by selecting the name of meeting in the chat section.

File sharing:

Files	Files shared appear at the top of the screen in the chat section for the meeting. You can view once uploaded and they remain for viewing after the meeting. You can always refer to these after the meeting by selecting the name of meeting in the chat section.

Be Fearless Test:
1. Select the calendar icon from the left side of the screen. A calendar screen will appear with "join" next to the name of the meeting name.

2. Confirm your video is on (you'll see a preview of yourself based on webcam settings) and phone is on. Select "Join Now."
3. During the meeting, use the mute option when you're not speaking to reduce background noise.
4. Use the chat option to paste a link or enter text. Select ▷ when you have typed your message to send.
5. To view meeting notes, select ▪▪▪ and select 🗒 Show meeting notes .
6. To view files, view the chat window on the right side of the screen during the meeting.
7. When the meeting is finished, select the hang up button.

 You can always adjust audio and video settings before you join a meeting. Select the ⚙ PC Mic and Speakers button before joining the meeting to confirm your audio speakers and webcam settings.

Chapter 4: Host an In-Person Meeting

I host and present during meetings in conference rooms for several reasons. I provide project status updates, present recommendations for discussion and decision, take notes for a team meeting or gain input from others on an initiative that I'm leading.

As I think of what's required for me to host a meeting in-person, I need a conference room sized for the number of people attending. I need a projection screen to show slides.

In reviewing how I could replicate this when working remotely, I notice that the meeting option is available in Microsoft Teams and I can share my desktop or a file with slides as I would if I were in a room. For those attending, video is available to replicate being in person. I've also noticed that Microsoft Teams offers a meeting notes area, keeping the meeting and notes together in a single place. I realize that this offers a viable alternate when in-person meetings aren't available.

Icons features overview:

 Your meeting invites scheduled through Teams. Your calendar may also appear here (e.g. corporate outlook calendar)

Join the meeting options:

Call options during the meeting:

	Video call show and hide. When a line is through this icon you are not showing video. You can show and hide video at any time during the meeting.
	Phone call audio speak and mute. When a line is through this icon you are muted. You'll often find words above this icon stating "your microphone is muted" when speaking while muted as a reminder. You can speak and mute at any time during the meeting.
	Share button. You can share a file that's already opened or your desktop. Be sure to open the file before you join your meeting to have it handy. If you're planning to share a Microsoft PowerPoint file, you will still need to select present once you share the file to ensure you are presenting in slide show mode.
	More options. This will be helpful to show meeting notes.
	The file share is available within the chat function. You can upload the file and a copy of the file will be available for all attendees during and after the meeting.
	Hang up.

Meeting Notes Function:

Notes ... Capture meeting objectives, important notes or action items	Meeting notes can be individual or grouped together. You can move a note up and down as needed and offer flexibility to differentiate between a note and action.
Meeting Notes	Meeting notes appear at the top of the screen in the chat section for the meeting. You can continue editing the meeting notes in this section once the meeting has ended.

File sharing:

Files	Files shared appear at the top of the screen in the chat section for the meeting. Attendees can view once uploaded and they will remain for viewing after the meeting.

Be Fearless Test:
1. Select the calendar icon from the left side of the screen. A calendar screen will appear with "join" next to the name of the meeting name.
2. Confirm your video is on (you'll see a preview of yourself based on webcam settings) and phone is on. Select "Join Now."
3. When ready, present your screen using the using the share button. Select the file you want to share, or

desktop to share your entire screen. If you plan to present a video or audio clip as part of the presentation, check ☐ Include system audio before making your share selection. You can repeat this step to switch between files if you don't want to show your desktop.
4. To show and enter meeting notes, select ⋯ and select 🗒 Show meeting notes. A pane will appear on the right side, and you can select "Take Notes" to begin taking notes.
5. To share a file, select the chat and the 📎. Select the location of the file and upload. Select ▷ when you have completed to send. Note: If your file is already located in a shared location, you can paste the link. If the file is a Microsoft filetype (e.g. PowerPoint) and it's located in Microsoft Teams it will automatically recognize the file in the window.
6. During the meeting, when you are not speaking, mute to reduce background noise.
7. When the meeting is finished, select the hang up button.

After the meeting, the title of the meeting will remain in the chat with comments and links that may have been added to refer to as you recap meeting notes.

Chapter 5: One to One Meetings

I have meetings with one co-worker at a time quite often. There are times when we need to brainstorm a process, or one person has a subject matter expertise that's helpful in a project and I can work with them outside of a larger meeting to optimize everyone's time. I also have progress check-in meetings with my boss.

As I think of what's required in a meeting with only one person, I need a whiteboard because we're thinking through a process and inevitably one of us ends up drawing. I need meeting notes to document ideas, updates and actions for next steps. And of course, we need a conference room with the ability to share the laptop screen because we both tend to share screens to navigate quickly.

In brainstorming how this could work when we're remote working, I realize that the meeting option is available in Microsoft Teams and includes video and desktop share options as I would if I were in a room. I also notice that Microsoft Teams offers a whiteboard and meeting notes area, so we can draw a process like we would in person and document notes for actions. The functions are the same, minus being in the same room.

Icons features overview:

 Your meeting invites scheduled through Teams. Your calendar may also appear here (e.g. corporate outlook calendar)

Join the meeting options:

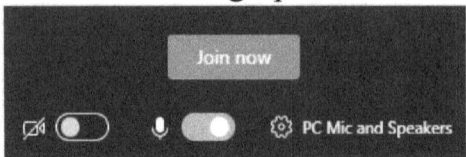

Call options during the meeting:

	Video call show and hide. When a line is through this icon you are not showing video. You can show and hide video at any time during the meeting.
	Phone call audio speak and mute. When a line is through this icon you are muted. You'll often find words above this icon stating "your microphone is muted" when speaking while muted as a reminder. You can speak and mute at any time during the meeting.
	Share button. You can share a file that's already opened or your desktop. Be sure to open the file before you join your meeting to have it handy. If you're planning to share a Microsoft PowerPoint file, you will still need to select present once you share the file to ensure you are presenting in slide show mode.
	More options. This will be helpful to show meeting notes.
	The file share is available within the chat function. You can upload the file and a copy of the file will be available for all attendees during and after the meeting.
	Hang up.

Whiteboard Function:

Whiteboard	The Whiteboard appears at the top of the screen in the chat section for the meeting within 1 more. You can always refer to these after the meeting by selecting the name of meeting in the chat section.

Meeting Notes Function:

Notes Capture meeting objectives, important notes or action items	Meeting notes can be individual or grouped together. You can move a note up and down as needed and offer flexibility to differentiate between a note and action.
Meeting Notes	Meeting notes appear at the top of the screen in the chat section for the meeting. You can continue editing the meeting notes in this section once the meeting has ended.

File Sharing:

Files	Files shared appear at the top of the screen in the chat section for the meeting. Attendees can view once uploaded and they will remain for viewing after the meeting.

Be Fearless Test:
1. Select the calendar icon from the left side of the screen. A calendar screen will appear with "join" next to the name of the meeting name.
2. Confirm your video is on (you'll see a preview of yourself based on webcam settings) and phone is on. Select "Join Now."
3. When ready, present your screen using the using the share button. Select the file you want to share, or desktop to share your entire screen. If you plan to present a video or audio clip as part of the presentation, check ☐ Include system audio before making your share selection. You can repeat this step to switch between files if you don't want to show your desktop.
4. To share a whiteboard, follow step 3 and select Whiteboard. The whiteboard will appear, and you can use the pen colors along the right to draw. When finished, select Stop presenting.
5. To show and enter meeting notes, select ⋯ and select 🗒 Show meeting notes. A pane will appear on the right side, and you can select "Take Notes" to begin taking notes.
6. To share a file, select the chat and the 📎. Select the location of the file and upload. Select ▷ when you have completed to send. Note: If your file is already located in a shared location, you can paste the link. If the file is a Microsoft filetype

(e.g. PowerPoint) and it's located in Microsoft Teams it will automatically recognize the file in the window.
7. During the meeting, when you are not speaking, mute to reduce background noise.
8. When the meeting is finished, select the hang up button.

 The chat thread with the meeting title will only appear if you have entered something in chat, created meeting notes, or if a file is shared.

Chapter 6: Hallway conversation

Hallway conversations are one of my favorite parts of the day working in the office. I have micro conversations on a topic to save thirty minutes of time sitting in a meeting. I have held decision meetings in the time it takes to walk to the next meeting. I use them as a heads up to inform for an upcoming meeting. And I use them for preliminary context to an email I'll send later in the day. I find these opportunities to be some of the most powerful options to use in my day.

I realize there's an art to them because it can equate to stepping on a landmine. Choosing too broad of a topic to solve for within a couple of minutes can have negative impacts. Knowing your audience, I've learned, is extremely important to avoid giving someone a heads up who is focused on their next meeting outcomes as you meet them in the hallway. In reflecting, I probably learned over time through trial and error.

As I stare at the remote box known as Microsoft Teams, I ponder possibilities to replicate this experience. Most of my hallway conversations tend to start with someone I am in a meeting with, or one I am walking with to a meeting. Chat could be an option to send an instant message for a heads up, and a call could offer an audio option for something that only takes a couple of minutes, which would equate to the time it takes to walk to the next meeting.

I test my theory the next day. I'm in a meeting that is ending 3 minutes early with the person I need to have a decision meeting with. I send an instant message saying, "Can we chat on this project for 2min?" I receive a yes. I dial to the person, ask my question to confirm moving a timeline forward and receive my decision. When I complete the call, I look at the time. We spent three minutes. I was 1 minute late for the next meeting, ahead of how late I usually am to the next meeting with the walk. Feeling more confident, I attempt more virtual hallway conversation replacements over the next week and learn this works!

Icon features overview:

	1:1, group Instant message chat threads. Meeting chat threads are also included in this section. A number in a red circle will appear when you have a notification for an unread chat.
	You incoming and outgoing phone call record. If voice mail is set up as part of your subscription it will be available here. A number in a red circle will appear when you have a notification for missed calls and voice mails.

Join the meeting options:

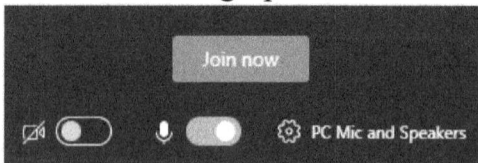

Be Fearless Test:
1. Select **Chat** from the left side of the screen.

2. At the top of the screen, select the ☐ for a new chat.
3. Begin to type the name of the person. You may see their name populate automatically. Select the name to confirm.
4. At the bottom of the screen, type your message.

   When complete, select the ▷ .
5. Once you receive a reply, use the phone options at the top right of the chat screen to call. Select either the "Teams call" or the phone number, if listed.
6. When your call is complete, press the hang up button.

Know your audience. If you are new to working remote and you've had successful in-person hallways conversations at the office with someone, continuing in a remote environment may prove to be successful. Everyone has different tolerance levels working remotely, and the company culture plays a large role. If remote working is a new muscle to build for everyone involved, give others time to develop it. People work at their own pace and may need time to develop remote working preferences.

Chapter 7: Open office space

I used to work in an open office space. There was always a buzz in the room with co-workers on phone calls and small talk. Over the years, the experience shifted to work at a desk in between meetings and move to a phone room for the meetings. When at the desk, my co-workers and I would listen to our favorite music on headphones and the phone calls and small talk moved to whispers because you can hear a pin drop in the space. Instant message became a norm for me to start a chat with someone I sat across from.

As I transition to a remote box trying to figure out how to replicate an open space environment, I have an idea. As a process, I instant message today using an emoji wave or stand and wave to the person to gain initial attention. It's followed by a move to a common area or a whisper conversation at the desk. In remote work, I can still begin by sending a wave emoji through an instant message. A phone call can follow up instead of in-person and I won't have to worry about whispering, which is good because I'm terrible at it.

Icon features overview:

1:1, group Instant message chat threads. Meeting chat threads are also included in this section. A number in a red circle will appear when you have a notification for an unread chat.

You incoming and outgoing phone call record. If voice mail is set up as part of your subscription it will be available here. A number in a red circle will appear when you have a notification for missed calls and voice mails.

Join the meeting options:

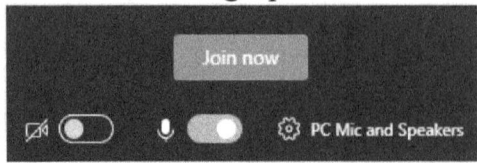

Chat options:

Emoji's and gif options are the most popular expressions in chat. Additional options including file share, text formatting, stickers, stream video links, praise and integrated options like Bing search and weather are available.

Be Fearless Test:
1. Select **Chat** from the left side of the screen.
2. At the top of the screen, select the [icon] for a new chat.
3. Begin to type the name of the person. You may see their name populate automatically. Select the name to confirm.
4. At the bottom of the screen, type your message. Within the message options, select the **smiley face** and locate the emoji desired or type wave and select your emoji. When complete, select the ▷.
5. Once you receive a reply, use the phone options at the top right of the chat screen to call. Select either the "Teams call" or the phone number, if listed.
6. When your call is complete, press the hang up button.

This is a great option to try with a team you work closely with.

Chapter 8: Coffee or Lunch breaks

I have casual meetups over coffee, and lunch with co-workers or my boss. It's perfect when I don't need to present slides and want to discuss a topic or update my boss on workstream that doesn't require impact decisions in a casual environment. I've talked through challenges and received fantastic advice through coffee and lunch breaks.

As I think about working remotely, I don't want to give up the value that a coffee or lunch session brings to my work life. And the thought of an audio call feels sterile. It had to be video and we had to bring our own coffee or lunch.

I tested Microsoft Teams with a meeting using the same title, and in the message area noted to bring your own coffee. I shopped for a mug with a funny saying. I went to the market and picked out fancy breakfast items.

I've noticed after a few of these that my relationships are closer. We've joked and bonded over the types of coffee or tea we prefer, our mugs with sayings, the fancy set ups we create for a fine dining experience and the food we choose (takeout is popular). We have learned more about one another even though we are talking by video through a remote box. It's a fun experience and one I've learned that I truly enjoy.

Icons features overview:

 Your meeting invites scheduled through Teams. Your calendar may also appear here (e.g. corporate outlook calendar)

Join the meeting options:

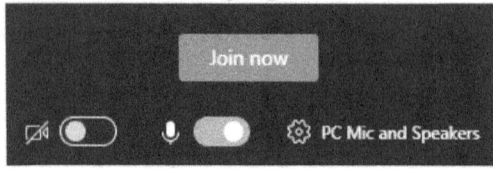

Call options during the meeting:

 Video call show and hide. When a line is through this icon you are not showing video. You can show and hide video at any time during the meeting.

 Phone call audio speak and mute. When a line is through this icon you are muted. You'll often find words above this icon stating "your microphone is muted" when speaking while muted as a reminder. You can speak and mute at any time during the meeting.

 Hang up.

Be Fearless Test:
1. Select the calendar icon from the left side of the screen. A calendar screen will appear with "join" next to the name of the meeting name.
2. Confirm your video is on (you'll see a preview of yourself based on webcam settings) and phone is on. Select "Join Now."
3. When the meeting is finished, select the hang up button.

Go overboard and don't be afraid to be ridiculous in the name of fun. This option offers the flexibility to order your favorite foods and enjoy your favorite drinks, so live it up and take advantage of sharing the experience. You may find you use your finest dishes more during these virtual coffee and lunch sessions than many years of use combined. Have fun with it!

Chapter 9: Morale Event

I've hosted and attended birthday celebrations, cooking events, work anniversaries and retirement parties over the years in the office. At each event I find there's a central reason to congregate and notice that it lightens everyone's mood with a break with a positive purpose during a chaotic day.

As I think about remote work, I couldn't imagine this is possible to replace. It's a moment of celebrating together with food involved, sometimes a gift is exchanged, memories are shared, there's decorations and if it's a birthday there's singing. But as I think deeply on it and stare at capabilities of Microsoft Teams, I realize that it can be replicated using an in-person meeting with light proactive planning.

I couldn't resist testing this. My teammate's birthday is upcoming, the person works remotely from us and we usually send a simple email with Happy Birthday wishes. I sent a message to the team letting them know that we would change it up and asked to pick a slice of our favorite cake and purchase a tabletop decoration for our desk. I also instructed them to pick their favorite celebration photo to use as a meeting background. I sent a cupcake and decoration to the birthday teammate working remotely.

As we celebrated the birthday with our teammate, it was incredible to watch. We joined an online meeting and started our video. Microsoft Teams has an option to add any photo background as part of the video call, and it was fun looking at the backgrounds everyone selected along with their tabletop decoration. I learned about my teammates favorite cake flavors, and we sang Happy Birthday. The celebration lasted fifteen minutes, and I received a message after from my teammate thanking me for one of their most memorable experiences. As I read the message of gratitude, I was thankful we recorded it to remind them throughout the year of how valuable they are to our team.

Icons features overview:

 Your meeting invites scheduled through Teams. Your calendar may also appear here (e.g. corporate outlook calendar)

Join the meeting options:

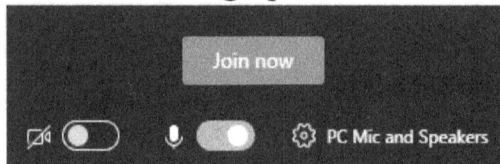

Call options during the meeting:

 Video call show and hide. When a line is through this icon you are not showing video. You can show and hide video at any time during the meeting.

 Phone call audio speak and mute. When a line is through this icon you are muted. You'll often find words above this icon stating "your microphone is muted" when speaking while muted as a reminder. You can speak and mute at any time during the meeting.

More options. This will be helpful to record the meeting and share your background. The background option is a newer feature, so double check if you have it. Microsoft Teams updates monthly, so if you don't have it available it should be over time.

 Hang Up.

Be Fearless Test:
1. Select the calendar icon from the left side of the screen. A calendar screen will appear with "join" next to the name of the meeting name.
2. Confirm your video is on (you'll see a preview of yourself based on webcam settings) and phone is on. Select "Join Now."
3. To record the meeting, select ▣ and select ◉ Start recording . A notice will appear at the top of the screen confirming recording for all participants.
4. To add a background, select ▣ and select ▣ Show background effects . A pane will appear on the right side, and you can select a photo or upload your own.
5. During the meeting, when you are not speaking, mute to reduce background noise.
6. When the meeting is finished, select ▣ and select ⌢ End meeting . This will stop the recording. Note: The meeting will stop recording when the last person ends the meeting, but if you are recording this you may

find that your video is longer than expected and dead space at the end. Selecting end meeting closes the recording when you select it.

 Challenge yourself on morale events. Try potluck lunches or any other creative option you can dream of.

Chapter 10: Best Practice Tips

I've compiled this list of best practice tips based on my own experiences and am sharing with you in case you find them helpful.

1. In-person meetings can make accents easier to understand than when working remote. If you are having difficulty understanding a speaker try using the captions feature within Microsoft Teams.

    - When in a meeting, select ⋯ and [CC Turn on live captions].

    - The captioned words (in your language based on initial selections when launching Teams) will appear at the lower left of the meeting.

2. Video calls make some people nervous. There's fear of being judged for not maintaining a clean space, and some people may not have a dedicated office space and will improvise using a dining table, kids craft table, sofa or other space. Try the following tips to feel more at ease.

    - Use the background in Teams to blur your background. When you join the meeting select [toggle] before you select join meeting.

    - Use the background in Teams to find a background photo. Select ⋯ and select [Show background effects]. A pane will appear on the right side, and you can select a photo or upload your own.

- You can always confirm your video settings before you join a meeting by using the `PC Mic and Speakers` option before you join the meeting.
3. Get dressed to the same degree you would going into the office. I've noticed that there's an increased sense of confidence in turning on video in calls as well as an increase in work from home discipline in people who are dressed in the same way I would see them in the office.
4. Meeting recordings are available through Microsoft Teams, and anyone on the call known as a presenter can record the meeting.
    - To record the meeting, select `...` and select `Start recording`. A notice will appear at the top of the screen confirming recording for all participants.
5. Working remote using Microsoft Teams allows some personalization using the top right of your screen for your profile photo, status updates and personal message.
    - Along the top right, select your initials (or photo If already uploaded). Select "Change Picture" `Melanie Gass / Change picture` and select the new photo.
    - Along the top right, select your initials (or photo If already uploaded). Adjust your status to busy, away or reset using the status options

- Available
- Busy
- Do not disturb
- Be right back
- Appear away

- Along the top right, select your initials (or photo If already uploaded). To add a personal message, select Set status message and enter your message. Messages can include your hours working, a personal quote or any other creative option you can think of. Your message is available to anyone who sends a chat message.
6. Making everyone feel included takes a small amount of extra effort when working remotely, especially on audio only calls as it's difficult to view the non-verbal cues you would normally see in-person. If you are the host of the meeting or presenting, look for moments to ask if there are comments or questions and confirm that everyone has expressed their point of view before you leave the meeting.
7. Microsoft Teams offers flexibility based on how we work remotely. This includes offering desktop, iPad, iPhone, Android apps for use. If you're on a web browser there's a web version of it.
8. The Microsoft Teams website has several training resources including a quick start guide and training courses to assist to get you started. When you look on the site, select resources. One thing I've found helpful is the knowledge check and on-demand trainings (they have live ones too) in the training course section. There's a lot of free training options available to you.

Want more?

Receive additional tips and learn more about Melanie Gass

Visit
Transformremotework.com

Notes

www.ingramcontent.com/pod-product-compliance
Lightning Source LLC
Chambersburg PA
CBHW052119070526
44584CB00017B/2558